INTIMATE
EXPRESSION

INTIMATE EXPRESSION

An Orphan's Experience of Healing

Dennis J. Dodt

Order this book online at www.trafford.com
or email orders@trafford.com

Most Trafford titles are also available at major online book retailers.

Printed in the United States of America.

ISBN: 978-1-4669-1191-8 (sc)
ISBN: 978-1-4669-1193-2 (hc)
ISBN: 978-1-4669-1192-5 (e)

Library of Congress Control Number: 2012900846

Trafford rev. 01/19/2012

 www.trafford.com

North America & international
toll-free: 1 888 232 4444 (USA & Canada)
phone: 250 383 6864 ♦ fax: 812 355 4082

CONTENTS

A MESSAGE OF ACKNOWLEDGEMENT

I acknowledge and thank all the truly amazingly gifted people below that have helped guide and support me throughout my healing journey.

Friends, Leo and Kathleen G. for their unconditional love, Brenda M. my fellow traveller and spiritual sis, Bill A. and Coral P. for their love and spiritual guidance when I was at a jumping off place in my life.

To my precious daughter Kelli you are a courageous soul. Thank you for teaching me so much about unconditional love.

I thank the many self help fellowships around the world for their acceptance and support of me. Members past and present Bill W, Dr.Bob S, Chuck C, Bob E, Jock M, Bill A, Barry T, Danny B, Ron W, Hilda and Robert S.

To the natural healers, spiritual guides, educators, role models, body-workers, writers who have helped release my hurts and pains on all the different levels of being. Rita W.B, Lars A., Cheryl K, Nikki N, Michael M, Robert K, Dr. Wendal R, Barbara B.

To thousands of people around the world I have identified with or guided I pray your life is a continued expression of the love that is in all of us.

To the many abusers from my past I want to say I forgive you. I pray you find healing and never abuse again.

INTRODUCTION

Living with Depression and not having a NATURAL way to heal and release Depression can lead to a very poor quality of life and a shorter life expectancy. In most countries the medical model is to visit a psychiatrist who will diagnose and medicate you with prescribed drugs for the rest of your life, which is very affordable with the Health scheme assistance. Or you can spend thousands of dollars on psychotherapy. The choice is not easy.

There is a great difference between the two methods—which presents a dilemma for the Sufferer of DEPRESSION who has to decide which method to use and which one to TRUST. I was diagnosed with Clinical Depression and told that I would have to be medicated for the rest of my life. Therefore there wasn't any need to look into the causes of my Depression. I was turned off to this approach, as it would make me dependant on drugs and the government, just to continue to survive.

This frightened me, so I chose to find a natural way to heal my Depression. This was not easy as it involved a lot of money, time, and commitment from me when I had limited money, no motivation, was overweight, fatigued every day, and had no job or income; not to mention a very untrusting attitude that stopped me from committing to anyone or anything. It wasn't easy.

In this book I have written all the tools, methods, and solutions that I have found that have helped me to heal myself and release my Depression naturally.

Having travelled the path to healing Depression myself, I have found that it is less expensive than I had first thought and a thousand times more beneficial to heal NATURALLY. It has only taken me 14 months of living the processes and methods I have outlined in this Book, to release my Depression and change my life permanently. I live today with more love, peace of mind, and quality of relationships than I ever dreamed possible.

I have spent the past twenty years healing myself of many things. Imagine being given the NATURAL SOLUTION TO HEALING YOUR Depression from someone who has the life experience to guide you? IT SURE WOULD HAVE HELPED ME WHEN I STARTED HEALING MYSELF.

THE MAJOR TURNING POINT IN MY HEALING JOURNEY

Five years into my healing journey the darkness of depression descended upon me once again. I came home from a self help meeting, followed by coffee afterwards at a local coffee shop. I was feeling very excluded from the group of people I had been mixing with for the past two years. One older man, with whom I had become very close friends with, and a person I looked up to as a big brother figure, really shut me out in that social setting. I felt hurt and rejected, angry and very confused.

By the time I arrived home, I began spiralling into a deep black hole of despair. I felt like I was going insane and feared that I was going to kill myself. I had never felt such bad feelings of mental torment and emotional pain before in my life. I was pacing backwards and forwards in my lounge room and not knowing what to do or who to turn to. I kept asking God for help and didn't seem to be getting any answers except the thought to ring a friend. I was in such a mess that I couldn't even see that this was God's answer to my prayer for help. I decided to give my friend a ring.

It was about midnight on a Saturday night. I felt scared that my friend was going to be mad with me for ringing so late and I also thought that because she knew the older man and the circle of friends that I was in pain over, she wouldn't want to help me. But as God would have it my friend was the answer to my prayer for help. She affirmed what I was feeling. We talked for about an hour on the phone and she said that what had happened to me was that I had been "Brain Fucked." I had never heard of this before but it really resonated with me and seemed to have a calming effect on my mind and my feelings.

After that night I began to really get into my emotional healing. I felt so grateful to this man and group of people because they had helped me start healing my emotional wounds. Therefore enabling me to grow up and not be so needy and co-dependent.

I can look back on this time and see how I may have been thirty-six years old physically, but I was like a newborn baby emotionally. I felt a little more personal freedom within myself at the time, which has continued to grow ever since.

My friend guided me as a friend and mentor for the next eighteen months, after which she died.

I was sent by my Doctor to a highly recommended Psychiatrist. I went there once and told him a little about my life experiences and at the end of our session he said that my brain was fucked and I would have to be medicated for the rest of my life. I felt abused by this so-called man of mental health, so I got up and said to him, "Do you mean to say that I cannot heal from the effects of my past abuse and that I will have to be medicated for the rest of my life?"

He replied "Yes."

I said, "What would happen if I was to take this medication and, say in about 10 years' time, and then decide to stop taking it?"

He said, "Oh! You couldn't do that."

I answered "So what about all the issues that have caused me to be in this state of mental illness, couldn't you help me with them?"

He told me that there was no need to deal with them, all I had to do was find the right medication to suit me and I would be up and running within four weeks, and able to go back to work.

I was shocked by his total inability to help me. I told him I wouldn't be coming back to him again. I believed that I could heal all the pains from my past and live some degree of happiness, and contentment in my life, without being medicated.

He said, as I was leaving, that he works with two thousand men and they are all treated this way and it works for them. All I could think of was those poor fellows and our poor society. Fancy our health system being run by so-called medical practitioners like this. Doctors such as this, in my opinion, are abusing rather than helping those in need.

Quiet a sad state of affairs.

This experience with the psychiatrist motivated me to get into action and start healing myself naturally. The beginning of my Emotional healing took me back to face my childhood—as it had a huge effect on my life and actually made who I had become.

My hope is that by reading this book you will be able to find peace in your own mental state. This is my story. Please read it and know that there is always hope. You are not alone.

Chapter 1

MY STORY

As I sit here typing, I recall a conscious dream that has been with me for most of my life—I see myself sitting on the ground on the hill of the orphanage, with my legs crossed and my elbows on my knees, and my chin resting in my hands. I'm waiting for my Mum and Dad to come driving up to take me home and I see my Mum reaching out to pick me up and hold me in her arms saying, "Dennis you're O.K. Son; you're not bad." I still dream that dream.

I am the 8th born child—born in the Central Queensland town of Rockhampton on the 11th of March, 1960—out of ten of us; I have five brothers and four sisters. We were a fairly poor family, but not an unusual fact for most of the people in our community. I lived a normal little boy's life, playing with the other kids in our neighbourhood. We played toy soldiers in the dirt, and made mud cakes, baking them in the sun, later pretending to eat them. I grew up with heroes like Ned Kelly and Captain Thunderbolt—a couple of famous bushrangers from our Australian History—Geronimo the American Indian, and Gandhi.

As a very young boy, not yet in school, I looked up to my older brothers, who made it look fun to slide down the hand railing of our house. As I was climbing up to the top rail I slipped and fell head first onto the concrete drain pipe; cracking my skull from one side to the other. (I still have a hole in my head from the incident.) My brothers, sisters, and several others from our street would also go up to the local Electrical shop and watch TV through the shop window. I only say this because in some ways, we were a normal family.

On my first day of school, wearing a white cotton shirt, I had been given a sixpence for my lunch. But on my way to school I saw a shop and decided to go in and buy a chocolate ice-cream. I managed to get the ice cream all down the front of my white shirt.

I went into the schoolyard to see two of my older brothers and ask them what I should do about my white shirt. They said "You are going to cop it when you get home for buying the ice cream and getting it all over your shirt instead of buying your lunch." This terrified me, as I remembered the beatings that happened to my mum. I decided to run away from school. I went and hid in the park with the Aboriginal wino all day until dark. I was scared and terrified of what my fate was going to be. On returning home that evening on my first day at school I never got into trouble.

The beatings, I am told, happened regularly to mum but I only have the memory of it happening once. Maybe my survival instincts kicked in and I started to live in denial of it happening. For instance, I remember there was a party in our back yard and all us young ones were made to stay upstairs and watch from the windows. Later I remember hearing my mum and dad yelling. I heard the sound of my mum's screams and furniture smashing. I was so frightened. I went over to their door and tried to help my mother, but I was only three years-old and I couldn't reach the door handle to get in.

My heart was breaking because I was not able to help my mum and stop her from being beaten.

When I do think of my younger years, I don't recall any memories of my mother or father ever holding me, hugging me, touching me, or looking at me with loving eyes; or even saying they loved me. My needs for love and attention came from somewhere else.

Whenever I was in emotional pain or needed some affection I would yell to the lady next door, "Lu Lu I want lollies." Sweets were what she used to give me to calm me down emotionally. If she wasn't home I would just have to live with whatever was going on.

Today when I feel fear, anger, sadness, hurt, pain, grief, or any other upset or conflict I still occasionally use sweet things to comfort myself. I have had to lighten up on myself for using sweets as an emotional coping tool; just as I have had to let go of so many other addictive substances over these last twenty years. This is a large problem for anyone to deal with when going into healing and recovery from childhood abuse, neglect and the associated depression.

I still strive for the need to be loved today and on rare occasions I still revert to using sweets to calm my emotions. Through my years of recovery and healing, I have come to see that I have been addicted to sugar as a coping mechanism for my emotional problems. This has been one of the hardest addictions that I have had to recover from.

As much as my younger years were an emotional roller coaster, little did I know how much the course of my life would change in the years to come.

Chapter 2

MY EARLY CHILDHOOD

My mother died and was buried on the 4th of March, 1964, seven days before my 4th birthday. No one ever explained to me that my mum had died, nor had anyone supported me through the grieving process. It wasn't until thirty years later, when I lost a close friend who had become a mother-like figure for me that I was able to heal from the effects of my repressed grief from my mother's death. I felt that my whole world was turned upside down.

For the first few months we lived out of town with our Uncle before being put into an orphanage for girls and boys. This was situated on the outskirts of Rockhampton. The Church, under the guidance of the State, ran the orphanage. I—and five of us younger children—was signed over to the care of the State and admitted to the Orphanage on January 3, 1965.

My father didn't have anyone to care for us while he was at work and he couldn't afford to support us.

I felt that there was something wrong with me. I felt that I was trapped within the confines of the orphanage, like I had been sentenced to a long-term jail sentence. I felt like I was a prisoner. That my Freedom had been taken away the day I was put into the orphanage. We weren't allowed outside of the orphanage grounds except to go to school, which was just across the road.

For the next two years, the six of us lived at the orphanage. Not everything was bad at the State School; I learned to walk on my hands with my brother, and my older brothers became altar boys for the church, which made me jealous to not have been chosen.

We used to have chickens and I remember feeling sick while watching the chickens get their necks broken in the hands of the older kids. Then they would chop the chickens' heads off and the blood would squirt out everywhere. I felt really sick at the site of all the blood. I still to this day have a very weak stomach whenever blood is involved.

I would play a lot with one of my older brothers and sometimes did artwork making a paper Mache' bird head that I could wear on my head. It was painted white and had black eyes and a yellow pointed beak.

For the most part, though, I felt lost; and that the other kids and adults at this school were treating me differently, now that I was in the orphanage.

After two years of being in the orphanage, we were put on a train to Brisbane where we were handed over to the people in charge of another church-run state orphanage in

Brisbane on April, 1967. Our lives were once again about to change.

By the time I had reached 7 years-old, I felt that my life had been pretty bad; I had been through my mother's death, separated from my dad and brothers and sisters, and still not knowing what happened to Mum. But as bad as it was, it was about to get worse.

The train to Brisbane was to be the last time I would see my two younger sisters for several years. My sisters weren't able to stay in the same orphanage as us because it was only for boys, approximately eighty of us. Instead, they were temporarily staying with my father and his parents

Upon arrival at the Orphanage my brothers and I were split up into what we were told would be our new family. I was introduced to five other boys, aged eight to fifteen years old, and told that these boys would be my new family. I felt shocked and scared and all alone, not knowing whom to turn too. The House parents sounded like very scary people. There were four elderly people who ran the house and looked after us; all eighty of us. There were two sixty year-old house parents, an old lady who was the cook, a middle-aged caretaker, plus a trainee policeman, who helped out when he could.

I had no idea that during the next two years, these House parents who were in charge, would put me through numerous abusive experiences.

My Life Was About to Become Hell

After having settled in to my new 'home' I realized that the life I had known before—which I thought was so horrible—was nothing compared to the life I was about to experience. I was threatened, punished, hurt and belittled.

One day I was forced to fight another boy until one of us could not stand. We were eight years-old and had been racing each other to see who would be first in line to go into the Gym. As punishment we were made to put on the boxing gloves and fight each other till one of us couldn't go on; if not, we would be flogged with the leather strap. I told the House parents that we didn't want to fight, and that I knew I was the best fighter so it wouldn't be fair.

So reluctantly, we fought. I had knocked my friend to the ground and he was pinned up against the concrete wall of the gym with blood coming out of his nose and mouth. I said that he was beat but I was threatened again with a flogging because they said that he wasn't flat on his back.

I asked my opponent to just lie down, but he was pinned against the wall in a corner. So I had to hit him again and push him to the ground without any luck. Then I turned to the House parents and dropped my gloves and told them I couldn't fight him anymore because he was beat and that they could beat me if they wanted; they flogged me with the leather strap.

Even though I won the fight I still felt bad; but on the other hand, I felt good because I had beaten the House parents by not continuing to fight when my friend was beat.

In second grade I won awards for being the best writer in the school, but because I was left handed I was told that I was being lazy. I had my left hand put flat on the desk and hit with a wooden ruler. Then they tied it to the chair behind my back and told me to write with my right hand and to stop being lazy. I felt so ashamed. I feared for my life, as I trembled using my right hand.

I kept getting into trouble for being so messy whenever I had to write. Thankfully the next year I was able to use my left hand.

My physical abuse was bad enough, but the torment and anger that I experienced was nothing compared to what I was about to experience; and that I would be unable to do anything about.

As if the torment and physical abuse I encountered at the new orphanage wasn't enough, I was now going to meet an abuser that would do more than that to me. The Police officer who was supposed to be caring for us came into my room one evening when I was asleep and started to sexually abuse me.

I was in total shock and terror with millions of sickening feelings and thoughts beginning to hit me from all sides of my mind and body; and I was not able to yell out for help because my of the fear of being flogged by the House parents. Plus, I was gasping for air while I was pinned down by my abuser with his penis in my mouth blocking my airways and I felt like I was about to die. I split off from my body and what was happening to me and went someplace else. I learned in healing that I had disassociated from my body. That helped me to survive the traumatising sexual abuse.

Eventually my abuser would let me be. I would lay there in shock and terror.

I had never been through anything like this in my life. This first attack really shattered my world and my trust in adults, especially because the sexual abuser was a Police officer; someone who is supposed to protect people from criminals.

It all started out so innocently. He would always have seven or eight of us on his bed in the afternoons playing with us, we took turns at sitting on his lap, and in what I used to think was just caring behaviour. Especially as all of us boys looked up to him as a safe adult role model.

For the next two years this abuse happened regularly. But I wasn't alone in this. I also saw this happening to other boys and I was always relieved that it wasn't happening to me. On the night after my first experience of sexual abuse I went to hide under the bed of one of my older brothers and I told him what the Police officer was doing to me. My brother was concerned for me and the flogging I may get from the House parents for making a noise, so he told me to get out from under his bed. I went quietly and hid under my other brother's bed without him knowing until my sexual abuser had left my dormitory.

I was living in constant fear of being sexually abused during the night and living throughout the day experiencing physical and emotional abuse by our house parents. Being publicly shamed every day while in public and at school forced me to shut down to the point where I felt like I was just an animal to be used and abused, whenever others wanted to.

Five of the boys who were being sexually abused decided to go to the House parents and tell them what the officer was doing to us. One of them volunteered to go first while the rest of us waited outside the office. We could hear the House

Parents going berserk at him, so we all panicked and ran for our lives. My mate copped a flogging every day for the next month for all of us.

Whenever I was found to have had wet bed clothes (from the sexual abuse), I was made to sit on the hot bitumen in the hot midday summer sun with my hands under my bottom, and my legs crossed with my wet bed clothes on my lap. While in this position, all 80 boys were marched past me under the angry voice of the House parents, saying that I was a dirty little animal. I felt so humiliated and ashamed of myself that I hung my head. Each time that I would hang my head one of the house parents would yell at me to lift my head, or they would flog me with the leather strap.

There were two other boys who had wet their beds copping the same treatment as me. But actually I had not wet my bed as they were saying—my bed clothes were wet from the sexual abuse that I had experienced from the police officer, and I believe this was also the case of the other kids.

Every day there were threats of being belted with the leather strap, but then we were belted anyway; if you were in the range of the House parents at the time. Living in constant terror of being belted at any time of the day, for little or no reason, was very confusing.

As the result of this continual sexual abuse, I lived with the nightmares of the Devil coming to get me, the moment I would close my eyes. I never got much sleep up until I went into foster care at the age of twelve where I discovered pills and alcohol. The move into foster care was initially on a temporary basis and then more permanently when I had settled in.

Chapter 3

ORPHANAGE YEARS

I never knew that my brother was also being sexually abused by the Police officer. I only found this out in 2002 when we were brought together with thirteen other boys to try and get a conviction against my sexual abuser, and my brother was one of them.

After four of us, now adults came forward we finally won the case against our sexual abuser and he was convicted to seven years jail. The sad thing about this is that he only has to serve seven years for crimes against at least fifteen young boys, when we have to live with the effects of what he did to us for the rest of our lives.

The Head Prosecutor said that because they had one conviction against this Police officer, they weren't going to pursue any of the other eleven cases against him—mine included. The reason they gave me was that the Police officer couldn't be charged again for the same crime.

They strongly advised me to drop my case because it would be highly unlikely to get another conviction on the same charges. It would also cost a lot of money to go ahead with my case and the other cases. I felt abused by the legal system.

I got really sick at the age of nine and had to be rushed to the Hospital with suspected Hepatitis but I recovered quickly. The House parents never believed us if we told them we were sick, so when we were sick, we would have to keep it to ourselves rather than get a flogging for lying.

I visited a World War 2 concentration camp called Shaushen-hausen outside Berlin in Christmas 2001 and I saw how forty or so prisoners were hustled and flogged every morning when they washed themselves and cleaned their teeth in a tiny wash room. It reminded me of how we were treated by the House parents.

It was the same only we were supposed to be living in a free civilized country where that sort of barbaric treatment didn't exist. I was handed over by my father to the care of the church as a State Ward and experienced a large amount of neglect and abuse, due to the minimal monitoring by the authorities into whose care I was entrusted.

Being made to stay in the orphanage when my father wanted to take us four boys out at age nine, was a big blow to my search for freedom. The house-parents said that whatever the majority vote was, from the four of us that would be the decision for all of us. My three older brothers didn't want go. So we all had to stay. This wasn't too bad for my older brothers as they wouldn't be in the orphanage for many more years. My brothers all had their own reasons for not wanting to leave the orphanage. Only one of them was being sexually abused like I was and none of them liked our father. I, on the other hand, still had at least six years to go; an eternity when you're only nine years-old.

Prior to our vote, we had been told by an older family member that our father had killed our mother and that was why we were in the orphanage in the first place. I think that this had a great effect on my brothers' decision to not go with our father. I also found out that I had four other older brothers and sisters that I didn't know about. It was at this stage in my life that I got to meet them for the first time. This was quite an exciting time for me. My siblings were all living and working in different places and had partners and lives of their own. I remember my second eldest brother giving us all a fifty cent piece that was so very precious to me. It was the first thing I had ever been given by anyone in my life. It made me feel special that someone valued me in some way.

In seventh grade I was one of the so-called toughest kids at school. I was a champion athlete and the best at cricket and football. Being a good cricket player I had been picked for the Brisbane squad. I was only able to go to training the first time because someone took me. But the next time I had no one to take me and I was dropped from the team. I tried to walk half way across Brisbane to make the training session, but I was too late. I didn't have the money to catch public transportation, nor the support of the orphanage.

One afternoon, after school had been let out and all the other boys had gone home, I was practicing cricket when another strange event happened. I went into the toilets and to my surprise I was greeted by two girls, much bigger than me. One of them was in my class and the other was her older sister, they were both fairly tall and big. Several days before, the girl who was in my class had wanted me to be her boyfriend but I wasn't interested, and I said no to her. Both the girls came at me and said that they were going to rape me. They both grabbed me and I started to fight back, but they managed to pin me to the ground and they both sat on me. I began swinging, kicking, and tossing and I eventually broke free.

Once out of the toilets I bolted home to the orphanage. Because of the shame of the attack, and the fact that they were two girls, I kept this to myself and never told a soul about it until I started my healing in 1991.

In seventh grade I took all of the boys out of school on strike because a teacher was shaming one of the boys for being fat and unable to read. Children's Services were called in, as well as the head of the education department and the school principle. The teacher was removed from the school. This you might think was a good deed for an eleven year old, but for me it wasn't. Mainly because nobody ever came up to me and said "Dennis we are so proud of you for doing this great deed for your fellow orphan, well done." I believe that this was just another example of the kind of neglect and lack of nurturing in my life.

Watching the other boys come and go from the orphanage made me jealous, especially when the boys who were placed in the orphanage for behaviour problems only stayed for three months or so, and then were let out. I would still be trapped within the confines of the orphanage. This always made me feel that I must be really, really bad.

There were a lot of fights in the orphanage for control, especially when a violent boy would be placed in the home for a trial probation period, before being released back into the community. One time a former golden gloves boxing champion was placed in our home who proceeded to bash up anyone who was considered tough, me included, until he was removed.

One source of my anger and shame came from the people in the public. We were constantly called "HOMEBOYS." Whenever anything went missing at school or someone was being bullied, or talking behind the teachers back, one of us would be blamed, or sent to the office for the cane, whether we did it or not. There was also that sinking feeling of shame when we were belted in front of other students by the House parents for not lining up in a straight line while being given our frozen lunch at school, or for no reason at all.

While the House parents were in charge there were always attempts to run away and escape from the orphanage; always without much success. The treatment the other boys got when they returned from an escape attempt was far worse than the treatment I was receiving in the home. I ran away with three other boys and was only able to get to the creek out behind the home before the fear of being caught got a hold of me and I decided to go back. The other boys went on and were all caught within the next two days. They were all flogged on their return and then transferred to an even worse orphanage.

Freedom, I always thought, was somewhere on the outside, but I have come to learn that Freedom is on the inside.

Chapter 4

FOSTER CARE

I took the opportunity at the age of twelve to be released into foster care until I turned eighteen; which was great since I could no longer stand being in the orphanage. I thought this would be a great move for me and that I would finally be free. But after I had been in foster care for only a few weeks I felt that I was still trapped and I still didn't have my freedom. The belief that I carried all through my time in the orphanages was that when I got out everything would change and I would be FREE. It wasn't.

My dream was shattered, I recoiled further into myself. I was out of the orphanage, but I couldn't stand it. I asked my older brother and my caseworker if they could put me back into the orphanage but they refused my request and I had to stay in foster care until I reached the age of eighteen and not before.

The next six years were very confusing for me, as I was going through adolescence.

My first couple of days at high school after being placed in foster care is when I was introduced to a couple of boys in my class and I thought that we were starting to get along when everything changed. I was sitting under a big fig tree eating lunch with one of these boys, the other boy came at me without any warning, I was hit in the head from behind. Both boys tried to get me to fight them, but I didn't fight back. I asked, "What was that for?" The boys said they had been told that I was tough because I had grown up in an orphanage. I said that I wasn't going to fight, and the boy could hit me again if he wanted and he did. I stood there in defiance and he got the message that he couldn't hurt me so he ended up shaking my hand and we decided to be friends from that point. I refused to fight him because of the time I was made to fight the boy in the orphanage. I thought that being out of the orphanage I would be free of the tag of being the toughest kid in the area, but it hadn't changed. A sad note to add here is that the boy who wanted to fight me hung himself several years later.

I guess the good thing that came from standing up to the boys was that I was given respect by most of the others at the school; once word got around about me standing up to one of the so-called toughs of the school.

There were a lot of gangs around in those days, with young teenagers becoming members. Once I had to beat up one of the weaker kids at school in order to prove my standing in the group I was mixing with. Fifteen years later this young boy was one of the first people I met when I started my own healing journey.

When I finished tenth grade I was forced to leave school and start working because my foster family couldn't afford to keep me unless I started to pay my own board and keeping. I took the first job I could find at the meat works, until I got an apprenticeship with a cabinet-making factory.

I was still not allowed to leave my foster home until I was eighteen years old, and I wasn't earning enough money to fully support myself.

My teenage years were just as screwed up.

I used to use rugby league to release some of my anger; it also gave me at least some social interaction with my friends. Rugby League was a great love because I could escape the reality of my life for a while. Although I was naturally gifted in this sport and many others, I never excelled because I would only use the sport as a social occasion and I wouldn't give it my all.

I began to use alcohol and cigarettes to help me cope during my time in foster care. Never having anyone I could truly turn to, or trust, was another source of pain for me. In the area of sex and girls, I had to lie and pretend a lot and this didn't allow me to have many lasting relationships or sexual experiences like most of my mates.

I always felt ashamed that when it came to sex, or having a relationship, I didn't have any idea of what to do with a girl.

I had a girlfriend during my later teens who I now know really loved me unconditionally. At the time, I couldn't handle anyone to love me that way because I was so screwed up. I found it very hard to maintain relationships during my teenage years. I still dreamed of the day when I turned eighteen. I would no longer be imprisoned as a State Ward. I would then finally reclaim my FREEDOM.

Chapter 5

FREEDOM AT LAST

My eighteenth birthday was celebrated with a party that ended in fights and me vomiting over the veranda several times during the night. It wasn't that big of a deal when the day came, no big party or jumping for joy or even much fuss was made by anyone. I was just relieved to be Free at last and not be controlled within an abusive State Care System for children. Several of my mates celebrated the occasion with me.

The day I left foster care and moved in with one of my mates. We were in this dump of a house that was lucky to still be standing by the time we left. I didn't mind, though, because my freedom was so important to me. There were constant parties because my housemate was an up and coming top footballer.

Our situation didn't last long because my housemate was not as keen about living away from the comforts of home life. So I was asked to go and stay with him in his family home. His parents were beautiful people, both hard working with three boys of their own around my age. Their eldest son had moved out of the family home and therefore there was room for me. The father loved sports and enjoyed fishing. Home life with this caring and supportive family was the closest I would get to a real family at this point. At this time in my life I felt very lost.

Girlfriends were still pretty scarce as I was too busy drinking, surfing and playing football to have time for them. Most girls would stay right away from me because I had this reputation as being very wild and out of control.

With a few drinks under my belt, I would become an Animal and nobody could predict what I would do at any given moment. Sometimes I would be the life of the party, or maybe an embarrassment, and sometimes I would cry; sobbing and wishing that my mum was there. Alcohol would give me temporary relief from the pain of living. I would turn up for work at the cabinet-making firm with my clothes on inside out—and still hung over, partly in a blackout. But I had such a good boss; he always felt sorry for me and I would manage to hold down my job.

These were turbulent years. My childhood nightmares were becoming more of a problem as each year passed. By the time I was twenty-two, I had this feeling that I would be lucky to make it to my thirty-first birthday and still be alive. I had a girlfriend who loved me, but that just scared me away. I was never able to maintain a relationship for more than three years. I have always felt that it has had a lot to do with my mum dying when I was only four years-old.

Not knowing how to communicate, I ended several relationships without any explanation. I just treated them badly because I felt they thought that I wasn't good enough for them. When I made amends to my first girlfriend many years later, she told me that I wasn't that bad, and that she could always see that I had a good heart underneath.

The beautiful thing about making amends with her was that in asking her sister to track her down, her family became reunited after many years without contact.

I struggled through these turbulent young adult years of having no one to turn to for help or guidance. I met and married a lady who was fifteen years older than me and had three teenage children. This suited me, as I could have the instant family life I had been desperately seeking.

During my years between eighteen and thirty-one I never had much contact with other siblings. Most of them lived in the same city as me but since we were never close while growing up, I never keep up contact with them.

During the ten years that my relationship lasted, we had a beautiful daughter, who I thought would make everything all right, but three years later the dreadful day came when my ex-wife took my daughter and left me. I didn't blame her for leaving me. I thought I would be married forever and that I would find security in the marriage, but this was not the case as my demons began to affect me more and more. I was living with more anxiety, depression, and stress as each day rolled by. I kept everything inside me hidden from the outside world.

My nights were filled with constant nightmares and I dreaded going to bed, except when I would have sex. Sex was always a way for me to be able to get to sleep at nights. This does not help with building a relationship. I could never talk in depth about this with my ex-wife because I was so immature. I didn't have the communication skills that I am only now slowly gaining, nor the self-esteem, or understanding that I do now. I would regularly take headache pills to try and ease the pain of these recurring nightmares and the feelings that came with them. I put my now ex-wife and her kids through a lot of emotional turmoil. I have been fortunate enough to be able to make amends to them over the last twenty years of my healing.

My nights would continue to grow into deeper and darker experiences of terrifying nightmares that I would keep to myself. The moment I would close my eyes the nightmares would appear in the form of a devil, with one eye and a large horn protruding from its forehead, which would come to get me and I would be smothered by this sickly feeling, and paralysed by the fear. I always felt that these dreams were somehow related to the sexual abuse and also the treatment at the hands of the house parents in the orphanage. My mind would start to spin out of control.

I would get so scared that I would have to wake myself up and try not to disturb anyone. I still lived with the terror of being belted by the House parents if I was to make any noise at night. I would try to stay awake as long as possible until I would fall asleep from exhaustion—normally getting three to four hours of sleep a night. It has been and continues to be a struggle to just lead some sort of ordinary life.

The effects from the abuse are scars; I will always have them no matter how much I heal. This has been a hard thing to accept. I am slowly dealing with it and after twenty years of healing I am getting dramatically better.

Whereas most people are able to live their lives focused on their careers and families, people who have been abused don't seem to have that choice. We are forced by the pain and torment of our childhood abuse and neglect to spend most of our lives focused on healing, just to stay alive.

I felt trapped when I was married and would think of ways out so I could be free again. I didn't have the capacity to get a divorce because of all the negative beliefs that I had accumulated through the course of my life. They were blocking me in so many ways. I wanted my freedom again but I was terrified that I wouldn't cope, so I was in a double bind. I was living on a diet of about sixty cigarettes, six to twelve cups of coffee, I drank so much alcohol on weekends I would blackout, I took prescription drugs for my migraine headaches, I was also working long hours and got three to four hours sleep nightly. I was 75kgs and getting sicker by the day.

I presented as the best father and man throughout my married life until the next major turning point in my life happened. For over a decade there were lots of good times with the family. There were also bad luck investments, occasional break-ups, and periods of excessive working to try and get ahead. I slowly began to lose contact with my brothers and sisters, and friends from school as I became more involved and committed to my wife, her three teenage children, and my own daughter.

I thought the birth of my daughter would make all the difference; and it did for a while. But it was just like when I got married, thinking everything would miraculously be all right in my life, but like everything that I did to fill that empty feeling within, it wouldn't last. I had spent thirty-one years of life trying to make that feeling go away, but without success. This, I believe, is why I turned to using substances and other things to distract me from facing my inner pain.

We lived in several different towns, moving from Brisbane to Rockhampton then back to Brisbane again when my daughter was born in 1987—moving twelve times in nine years and working many different jobs along the way. I have never had a place that I could call home and this has been a source of pain throughout my entire life. One of my dreams is to someday have a place I can call home where, "Love is FREE to grow."

After breaking up and getting back together several times with my future wife, we eventually got married. We brought a house and tried to make it into a home but I wasn't successful at it. At the time I didn't know just how screwed up I was from all my past childhood abuse and neglect, and how much it was affecting my life.

I lived in fear that the stress would bring on a heart attack. The medication never seemed to work; my feelings and my mind were racing out of control. "Freedom" still eluded me, even though I was outside of the care and control of the State. I was more confused and frightened than ever before.

Fear of Fear gripped me and the darkness fell upon me and there was no apparent way out.

Chapter 6

MY HEALING BEGINS

I started to see a counsellor three times a week and went to a support group once a week, which dealt with co-dependency. I went to see a couple of psychiatrists and I also visited a Drug and Alcohol treatment centre. After identifying with so many addictions; ranging from Alcohol, work, sex, love, gambling, prescribed drugs, cigarettes, caffeine and several other unhealthy coping mechanisms, I sat down one night and said to myself, "God where do I start?" I didn't believe in God at the time but I think that when anyone genuinely asks for help from whatever source they believe in then the tumblers in the wheel of life seem to click into place and miracles begin to happen.

I remember that voice, deep within my mind saying, "Ring your support group counsellor," and I did. She asked me, "What do you think is your major problem?"

I said "Alcohol.

She replied, "Why don't you go to a self help group that deals with alcohol problems?"

Upon hearing her say this, the voice in my head said "Oh your brother-in-law is a member of that why don't you give him a ring and see if he can help."

So I hung up and felt a little hope start to come into my life. I rang him straight away and he said that he would take me to a meeting the next night.

This is when my journey into spirituality began and continues to this day.

I started going to these meetings every day and also to other twelve step fellowships. These groups gave me an outlet to talk about my problems. It enabled me to get the support I needed in healing my addictions and cleaning up the mess that I had made of my life

Finding Help.

When looking for help I would ask the questions and gather the information outlined at the end of the book; for all my therapists/ counsellor/ spiritual guides/ life coaches / mentors/ sponsors I used to help me heal myself.

Upon sitting and listening at my first self help meeting I found that I was not alone, nor was I so different. I sat and listened with everything I had. I was desperate for some answers. When I listened to the first six people share their stories, I had never heard anyone share so much truth about themselves before, especially not to an audience. I didn't identify with the drinking nearly as much as I related to the people and how they felt, and what I could see in them.

I saw one man who looked very tough but all I could see in him was his Insecurity; then there was another man who I thought had a big Ego. As I looked around I saw another man my age who looked angry and arrogant. There was also another man I went to school with and I even remembered beating him up at school. He came over and talked to me and I noticed how frightened he looked. He made me feel welcome and at ease.

What I didn't know at the time was that all the things I could see in these people were a reflection of me. After about six people had shared their stories, I was asked to share. I thought that I was going to tell them my story, as it looked easy, but I hadn't experienced the power of identifying with these people; that was what I was about to experience.

When I got to the front and identified, I experienced a huge out-pouring of emotions. I wasn't able to say another word; I just stood there and sobbed and slowly went to the back of the room and sat on the steps and lit a cigarette. I felt like I had come home.

I went to self help meetings every day for the next three years and got heavily involved in both the program and the fellowship. My addiction switched to meetings, which I believed was okay for me as that was what I needed. I was so screwed up on all levels: spiritually, emotionally, mentally and physically, I wasn't sure if I was animal or human, male or female, sane or insane, or even if life was worth living. Thankfully this first meeting put me onto the path of recovery and healing.

For the first seven weeks all I could do was go to meetings every day and sometimes three meetings a day if I needed. I would work for eight hours a day when I was up to it, reading literature or talking with people, and listening to tapes all to keep me from killing myself or going insane.

At the seven week mark of attending meetings, I felt worse than ever before—suicide was looking like my only way out—I thought I would have to go away and do the program just to keep from doing that.

I took eight days off from work for a holiday. I booked a unit at Palm Beach on the Gold Coast. The fears, paranoia and sleeplessness set in and intensified. I went to meetings three times per day and met with members' in-between for the first four days. I had gotten to a point of total and absolute desperation where I felt I couldn't go on living anymore. I would stay in my unit all alone, in so much emotional pain and mental torment that I said one of my first genuine prayers. "God please help as I cannot go on; please put someone there to show me how to change." I thought to myself, if that doesn't work then I can kill myself.

Thankfully my prayers were answered and I went off to sleep for the first time I could remember. I slept through the night like a baby. I awoke with this strange feeling that someone was going to be at the meeting to help me with the program and that everything was going to be O.K. I didn't know how it was going to be O.K, but that didn't matter.

I went off to a self help meeting that I had been attending and there I met this big American who I had met the day before. He had this big smile on his face and I asked him if he would help me and show me how to do the program and he said yes. He said that he had five hours to spare and that if I went and got my notebook and then we could start straight away, so I did, and we got started.

During this first seven weeks I also was going to counselling three times per week, to my co-dependency support group once a week, several self help groups as often as I could. On top of this I was at my doctors every two weeks using lifeline phone counselling daily in the early hours of the morning, making occasional visits to different psychiatrists, regular visits to my older sister's place due to emotional breakdowns, smoking sixty cigarettes a day, drinking twelve cups of coffee per day, not eating very often, and taking migraine tablets and other prescription drugs. I was not in a very healthy state.

FINDING PEACE WITH MYSELF

As my new-found American friend guided me through the self help program, I felt like I was being possessed by something out of my control. We spent the afternoon going through the first three steps. I went off to my unit and I began to write out my life's troubles. I was filled with new power and energy. I felt wide-awake and not fatigued like I had been.

I had a flash of light-spiritual experience before I started writing. I saw the whole world in front of me stop and I then felt a perfect peace and calm within myself like I had never felt before. Then I started to write, going back through my entire life and by the time I was finished it was about three a.m. I had written for about seven hours straight. I had written some fifty pages about my life, then it stopped all of a sudden and I went off to sleep.

The next day I went to my American friend and he guided me through the next part of the process which was to do with my sexual experiences.

When I had finished my writing I met up with him that afternoon and we went through what I had written down. When we had finished we jumped into my car went to get something to eat and drink.

My American friend was laughing at me while I drove the car and I told him I felt very strange, like I was not in control of myself anymore. He told me "That is natural; it will last for about six months." I didn't know what he meant, but I sure felt good inside myself. I felt like someone else was driving the car, that I was now taking a back seat. I was beginning to have a spiritual experience and I later came to understand that this is what was happening to me. He was right about this spiritual experience lasting for about six months—I actually experienced it for about fourteen months. Lots of strange and unusual things began to happen to me.

I began to have this permanent grin on my face, which I couldn't stop even if I tried to. I felt this new power flowing in and through me. I remember stopping at a garage to get something to eat and drink; some BBQ chips, chocolate, a bottle of soft drink, and a pack of cigarettes. At the time these were my favourite things. When I began to eat the chips I was revolted at the taste. I tried the chocolate and the same thing happened; and again for the soft drink and cigarettes. This puzzled me and I had to go back into the shop and find out what I did like. This was making me feel really weird.

I went with it—not understanding what was happening to me. I ended up walking out of the shop with a bottle of water and some fruit. When I tried to smoke, as I was about a 60 cigarette a day smoker at the time, I choked and coughed until I got my breath back. I couldn't, eat, drink or smoke, or put unnatural or unhealthy things into my body anymore, even if I tried.

Even my prescribed headache pills for migraines didn't work for me anymore. All of this, I now know, was to be a part of my spiritual wakening. I began to experience Peace of Mind for the first time. This scared me a little, until I got some feedback that this was normal when anyone went through the steps as I had. Especially after I had purged all of the past thirty-one years of pain, hatred and suffering from myself.

I started to get answers to everyday problems from all sorts of unusual places like trees, animals, and my meditations. My senses (hearing, smell, touch, feeling, intuition) became more alive and alert. I didn't seem to be in conflict with myself anymore. I was at Peace with both the world and myself, at last. During this time, there were so many miracles and they have continued to happen in my life and still do. Finally I was beginning to feel the Freedom I was searching for all my life.

I went back to my unit and did everything the program asked me to do. I then prayed. When I got up off my knees I went and sat down at the dining room table and looked out of the balcony glass doors towards the ocean.

As I was looking out the doors, I saw out of the corner of my eye a dark image (a shadow) walk from my bedroom to the spare room. This scared me, so I jumped up and called out, "Is anyone there," with no answer. I kept calling as I looked thoroughly through both bedrooms; under the beds and in the built-ins, but nobody answered. I felt a lot lighter within myself. I calmed down emotionally.

I had this realisation that this dark shadow was the dark side of me leaving me. My dark side was losing control over me. I had had this creepy dark shadow and associated feelings for as far back as I could remember. It would visit me every night and this was what had been stopping me from sleeping peacefully.

I continued through the rest of the program.

After a later weekend away with many hundreds of other people I made many new friends with. One of these new friends was an old mate from my teenage years. A new life began to come into view. Then when I was on my way home all the colours in the world appeared to be richer and more vibrant. I felt like I was in a new world, everything appeared to be different and strangely new to my eyes.

MAKING Peace with my past

I started to pray for those I had to make peace with in my past. On every occasion I would find the answer to how to make peace, either in the literature or from someone I would run into. Miracles regularly happened in my life. Living this new spiritual way of life I started to become much more happy and peaceful with myself and with the world around me.

I went to my ex-wife first; I shared with her what I was doing and apologized to her for all that I had done; for all the pain that I had caused her and her family. This went extremely well and we began to get along better. I didn't even know what love was anymore. So we stayed apart. One good thing is that we are still friendly towards each other.

I made peace with my first girlfriend—which was another miracle that I could make my peace with her. Plus the bonus for her was getting back in contact with all her sisters as they hadn't seen each other for eleven years.

My dad was the next person I had to make peace with. When I went to him he was drunk after being on a bender for two weeks; he had slowly become a chronic drunk after my mum died. I went to his unit to make my peace with him. I forgave him for what he did to my mother when I was three years-old; I forgave him for the fact that he was an alcoholic; I forgave him for putting us into the orphanage and for not being there for all of us as we grew up.

The real significance in what I had said was calling him Dad for the first time in my life. He started to cry. I stood up and went towards him. As I got up to go to him to give him a hug I said "I love you." This was the first time in my entire life that I had ever said "I love you" to anyone and really felt it.

As I held my arms around him he said that he always knew that one day one of his 10 children would come, but that he never thought it would be me. We built a little bit of a relationship over the next three years before he died. At his funeral I had a feeling that his spirit was with me. I felt that I had said all that I had wanted to say to him before he died and this gave me more peace and contentment.

Making peace with the man who sexually abused me as a young boy was another miracle. I was about two years into living the new spiritual program and I was working away peacefully. Then all of a sudden I got this over-powering urge to go home and find him to make my peace with him. I had only an hour to go till I was finished work for the day but I couldn't wait; the feeling kept getting stronger until I decided to go home. I prayed about this and then started to make some phone calls and, to my surprise, within about fifteen minutes I had his contact number.

I tried it but no one was home. I waited another hour and got through. I was able to offer him forgiveness for what he had done to me even though he tried to deny it ever happened. He said he didn't even remember me but he gave himself up by asking me how my brothers were doing. He knew them by their names. I felt that I had received the acknowledgement I wasn't even looking for. I came away from this phone call with the feeling that I had been forgiven and that the feeling of forgiveness was now in me.

I had many other miracles in healing relationships over the past twenty years and one thing I have learned about making peace with others is that when I make peace with someone in my life, I feel like I am gaining more peace with myself.

There have been a lot of people that I have had to make my peace with over the years. These are just a few.

After three years of living at Nambour I was starting to die, spiritually, on the inside and was encouraged to move back to Brisbane to help with my spiritual growth. So I moved to Slacks Creek to live and work.

For the next two years I tried everything to try and fix my growing emotional depression without any success. During these two years I was fortunate enough to become close friends with an older lady who was to become a close friend and mentor until she died in 1997.

In the end, I decided to quit my job as a cabinet-maker and to have some time out from the pressures of life. I couldn't mentally or emotionally work anymore. I lived on the $13,000 I had in my savings account until my money began running out and I had to go and see my doctor.

I was suffering from what my doctor said was a case of Depression, Stress, Anxiety and Fatigue. I needed time off from life in general. So I took his advice and went on a three-month sickness benefit and I began to heal my emotional pains. At this point I was planning on going to America to do my healing, but God continued to send the helpers I needed. I was almost completely financially broke, mentally and emotionally screwed, and physically 20kilograms over weight. I had stopped smoking for about two years, had no debts, but just surviving on the last of my savings.

Looking through the phone directory I was guided to the first person I felt drawn to and called him. He said he couldn't help me but he had just received a letter about a man who would be coming from America in five weeks' time to run a four day workshop that might be good for me. At that point, I wanted to try anything that might work to make me feel good again.

Chapter 7

EMOTIONAL HEALING

I have this feeling that I am a warrior of the old school and my experience in this life is to heal emotionally. I also feel that I have been given this gift of WILLINGNESS to face my pains, past and present. To be an example of how one can return from living in Hell with Fear and Torment being my constant companions, to living with Peace and Love and Joy.

The five weeks passed quickly for me while I was waiting to do the four day Emotional Healing workshop.

I met the facilitator at the beginning of the workshop. I was a participant and so was one of my close friends. I also met a lady I had known from my school days and she was doing her training in the work within this workshop.

At the start of the workshop I was triggered into some original pain from the tone of the facilitator's voice. It reminded me of the house-parent in the orphanage. I regressed back to that state of being a little boy aged about seven years-old and I felt very scared that I was going to be belted if I made a noise. I spoke up to the facilitator about this and he said for me to put my hand on the part of my body where I was feeling the pain. I did this and put my hand on my heart. He said for me to sit with the pain and say what comes up.

I started to sob loudly and uncontrollably. He walked over to me and acknowledged my pain and this made me feel like he really cared about me. This other guy was triggered as well, but the facilitator worked with him differently than he did with me. I was feeling my feelings but the other guy wanted to just stay in his anger and not go into his feelings. The facilitator told him to sit with his anger then he went back to running the workshop.

I went into my original pain several times during the next four days. I woke up in the morning on the second day in my motel room, all alone. I had been in intense pain through the night and tracking a belief that *"I hated myself."* I caught a glimpse of my face in the corner of the mirror opposite my bed. I started to cry as I began to feel that *"I liked me,"* which is the positive belief that I was working through during the night. It was only for a brief moment that I felt this new positive belief, but that feeling is still with me today and is growing with every day.

On the last day of the workshop, as we were about to go home, I started to sob uncontrollably and the facilitator asked what that was about. I said that I was afraid to go home because I had no one there to greet me and this reminded me of how I had felt all my life. There was nobody there for me. Then, while I was sobbing the facilitator came over to me and sat in the vacant chair beside me, he put his arm around me and held me while he continued talking to the rest of the group. I now really felt that another human being not only cared for me, but that he also loved me like I had never been loved before. This made me sob even more. I felt like my life was just beginning for the first time. Here was the first person who not only helped me and showed me how to work through a process to heal emotionally, but he physically showed me how I could be unconditionally loved back into good health as well.

I knew that I couldn't become dependent on this man, as he was going back to the USA in a couple of days. I needed to connect with some of the people from the workshop for my ongoing support. This is when I connected well with several other participants. I had also heard that another therapist in the workshop was training in the work as well, so I asked her if I could go into one of her support groups to continue practising the work, so that I could train in this work for myself.

My friend who had come with me said that she had found the answer as to why she had created the cancer that was now killing her. My friend said that this is what all people needed; to grow emotionally. We talked about how we could give this to other people for a lower price. I decided to continue with my own healing for the time being and see what comes from helping others in the future.

I went into group work for the next five school terms to reinforce my learning of this process. I started to let go of a lot of negative beliefs over the next eighteen months. I felt like this was my purpose in life, to heal naturally. To be drug free, healthy and whole just the way I was born; only now I was an adult.

I processed about one to three beliefs a day for nearly the whole year until I came to a place when it all stopped. I noticed that I wasn't getting triggered all the time like I had been before. My depression, anxiety, fatigue, stress, sleeplessness, and weight problems all started to leave me permanently. I felt very strange as this new state of BEING began to grow and grow. I started to laugh and learn how to play again. I began to be spontaneous again with a free-flowing spirit.

At this point in my life, I started working on my inner-child with a male therapist. I met him twice a week for five weeks until I felt that I had done all I could do with him. He helped me to see where I was; developmentally. I was at age zero and beginning my learning of TRUST verses MIS-TRUST. He also helped me to re-integrate the three parts to myself—the Adult, the Child and the Parent. This was very powerful work and it complimented the belief work. I also was doing my debriefing in the Male Abuse and Rape Survivors support group while I was in the belief support group.

I finished the support groups when I decided to do a seven day workshop plus a seven day holiday in Bali. Several therapists and other practitioners were going to guide a group of about thirty people through a process of finding out what our purposes were in life and also to re-visit the belief work process.

This was also a part of loving me and celebrating my journey in natural healing so far.

Chapter 8

FACING MY FEARS

I was sitting at the airport feeling nervous about the seven hour flight from Brisbane to Denpasar, Bali. This trip would be twice the distance of any flight I had taken before and the second major trip of my life. On this trip I would be a lot more supported than when I went to New Zealand. I sat on the plane with a business-man from the Gold Coast, so I had someone to talk to about how I was feeling.

I met the man from the Gold Coast just before we boarded the plane; I shared with him how I was feeling very nervous and scared about flying, being in a confined space and not being in control of the flying of the plane. He wasn't very supportive of me and this pissed me off. I felt that because he was doing the same workshop, he should have been emotionally mature enough to be able to acknowledge my feelings, but he wasn't able to. I decided to keep expressing my feelings anyway and this helped honour the little boy inside of me.

I was also going to be meeting up with several other people who were doing the two weeks in Bali with me. The biggest thing about this trip was that I would not be doing it all by myself. I wouldn't have to go through those awful feelings of being alone and feeling lonely.

I managed to handle the flight and arrived in Denpasar on Friday afternoon. It was hot, humid and sticky. There were so many people everywhere and as we started on our trip to the town of Munduk (where we would be doing the seven day workshop), we were confronted with thousands of Balinese people protesting on the streets, and there were two opposing groups fighting. Our driver said not to worry, as we would be able to drive the bus through the rioters.

I felt really scared that we might get caught up in this riot and that I might get killed. Thankfully the driver was right, we were able to push our way through the rioters and drive on up to Munduk. We arrived safely in the mountain town of Munduk just before dark. There was some mix up with our accommodations at the Retreat when we arrived, so this Irish Javanese Priest and I had to spend the first night in a home-stay with one of the villagers. I didn't mind this and I felt that it was an honour for them to take me into their home for the night.

They were very poor people in the material sense and their standard of living was much different than ours back in

Australia. No power, hot water or taps with running water, no toilets, fridges or the things that I take for granted back home.

I felt excited about being in Bali and also scared that I was about to embark on another Spiritual Quest. I was also feeling very tired by the time I went to bed that first night, but thankful that I had arrived safely.

Getting to know me better

I awoke to the strange sounds of dogs and music coming from a Gamelan, a traditional Indonesian musical instrument and very loud. I would go for exploring walks every morning with the Priest, all over the area. Pat helped me to learn to speak Balinese and we had lots of beautiful experiences on our walks.

After breakfast we moved up to the Village Hotel where the rest of the group was and also where the workshop was going to take place. I was sad that I had to move as I was really enjoying the stay back down in the village.

I was shown up to the room that I would be sharing with another person. It was a beautifully built and crafted, colourful two bed Balinese hut overlooking the valley below. As the workshop was about to start I didn't have time to unpack as I had to get back to meet up with all the people in the workshop. I met some people I knew and I was introduced to all the rest of the group.

We met all the facilitators and were told that the main facilitator was not able to make it for the belief part of the workshop. I was disappointed as he was the main reason that

I wanted to do the workshop. The workshop co-ordinator said he would create something in the time that was left vacant, as the workshop unfolded.

I talked with another participant about a negative belief that I needed help with; it had been triggered by my roommate. He was so negative. He had so much knowledge about spirituality and life, but it was all in his head and I found him to be very draining on my energy. After working through my belief I had to talk with him about my needs to have my own space and privacy.

My roommate didn't seem to understand my needs and the boundary that I was placing on him. I had to just let it go. I decided that for my own well-being I would have to continue to set boundaries with him while I was in his company; it was too much for me, or I could always change rooms. I was very thankful that I had met him, as I learned so much about myself over the course of the seven days of the workshop. I did enjoy some of the books that he had brought with him on spirituality.

I met up with some very beautiful people in the workshop, who I connected with. We spent the first day of the workshop getting to know each other and we did several joining activities, starting the process of going through the workbook that was supplied. We would all meet for our meals in the main eating area around the raised floor workshop space overlooking the valleys on both sides of the hotel.

By the end of the day I felt like I was beginning to get to know all the participants. The meals and service were excellent and I felt that I was being treated to luxury for the first time in my life—and the feeling of being nurtured was very strong for me.

I booked a 1 hour bodywork treatment with an old lady from the village for the next night. It made me feel very appreciative of my home because I had to cart a bucket of water to use for my shower. I had to wet my body with a cup for the water and then soap myself up, then throw cups of cold water over myself to wash the soap off. I didn't take too long with this washing, as it was so cold.

After dinner and my shower I went down to where the villagers were putting on a traditional Balinese Dance and Music performance, especially for us. I felt so privileged to be experiencing this. I got to sit at the front and was amazed at the beauty of the dancers. I was even more amazed when I was picked out of the audience, with a woman from our group, to get up and dance with the main woman in the dance group. She showed us how to do a traditional dance. I was so excite to be able to dance with these people and felt honored to be chosen by the village people. This feeling increased when I was told that we were some of the first people to ever be allowed into this particular village.

I went to bed with the feelings soaring through my body; about where I was and what I was doing. I was able to make some space for myself back in my hut with my roommate. I felt like I had to be cold towards my roommate just to get him to respect my personal space, so I could have the quiet time I needed to meditate and write in my journal.

My heart breaks free.

I awoke after a restless night and my emotions were all over the place. I went to see two other therapists attending the workshop about some beliefs that were triggered by a lady in the workshop. The beliefs were, *"I am unattractive,"* *"I am undeserving of Love,"* and *"It is wrong to express my Love."*

After working through these, I made the decision one day to face my fear and share how I was feeling with a lady in the workshop during the lunch break. At the start of each day in the workshop we would share what was going on for us and how we were feeling. When it was my turn to share I felt a lot of fear and other emotions coming up in me. I stayed with my feelings and shared with the group.

I started sobbing and tears were pouring out of me, when all of a sudden I felt the hard shell that was surrounding my heart, begin to crack open and the tears continued to rush out. One lady was beside me and she instinctively cuddled up to my heart and my therapist friend put her arm around me on the other side. A male friend and several others in the group came and surrounded me with their arms and there love, supporting me with a group hug and silence until I stopped sobbing.

We would have many great experiences like this throughout the whole of the workshop. We did some activities that helped us all to identify our Totem animals. A totem animal is an animal personality that you can see in yourself and others; in their unique qualities, the ways they walk and conduct themselves in their life.

You either resonate with them or you don't. If you do resonate with a particular animal then try looking at their behaviour and ways of being. See if they resonate with you, and if there personality is like your own personality and ways of being.

I was amazed at how, after I did these activities, I could clearly see everyone's totem animal and felt connected to my own, which is the Tiger. The Priest and another two ladies were also Tigers.

After lunch we did some more work sharing our discoveries about our Totem animals, then had a briefing on what we would be doing in our men's and women's groups for the next two days.

I felt like I was being infused with love from within myself and I didn't fully understand what was happening to me. I had a mixture of feeling fear and not knowing, plus outbursts of emotions of absolute joy, peace, contentment and love. Not only for other people, nature and animals, but for myself as well.

I felt that I was going through a transformation from one level of being and consciousness to a much higher level of feeling and awareness. I am still growing and expanding with each passing moment.

As I parted from the ladies I began to feel sadness around not seeing them for the next couple of days.

I was asked by the workshop co-ordinator if I would be interested in running the men's group in the next couple of days. I said that I felt honoured to do this even though I had never done something like this before. He said I would be good at it and that he knew I would be able to do it. I felt even more honoured as another older man I respected agreed with him about me being the facilitator for the Men's gathering.

Peace with myself again

I prayed and meditated about this for most of the night and the next morning. I had to digest and work through the emotions and thoughts of Love, Joy and Peace within myself. I was also feeling overwhelmed and stressed about what I was going through, but for some strange reason I felt capable of handling it all. I felt like I was protected by the power of my Totem animal, the tiger, and that the energy of the tiger was with me in all that I do.

This was a strange new feeling and power. I sensed that the qualities and ways of the tiger were the same qualities and ways that I was moving with in this world. As I was walking on the path back to my hut I had a very strong realisation that I was one with the power and energy of the Tiger. This realisation and growing power really comforted me.

After I had dinner and a bath I had a timely massage booked with one of the old ladies from the village. The massage was so revitalising and cost only $25Aus. I felt that the massage helped me to work through some of the beliefs that one of the ladies had triggered in me which was; I am unattractive, unlovable, and undeserving of love. I also felt that it was a good way to nurture all that I was discovering about myself, as well as all the transformations that were happening within myself.

I sensed that the feelings the massage was bringing up for me, sexually, were feelings that I would have to get used to and somehow allow being present in my body. I felt that these were some of the disconnected feelings and power that I had shut off due to my sexual abuse I had experienced as a child. I was now reclaiming this power and these energies for myself and believed that this was the beginning of true Intimacy and true Love.

I am still amazed at how God arranges for all the right people and situations so we can release and resolve problems from our past, and so we can live in harmony with ourselves and the world around us. My Depression, Fatigue and anxiety were slowly lifting, more so in Bali than ever before.

Chapter 9

LOVE AND INTIMACY

I still feel to this day that I am learning how to live with someone unconditionally loving me. I am learning what that is supposed to be and feel like, as I have never experienced it.

I was living with my best friend and his wife at this time, working through my beliefs. These two people love me unconditionally and have helped me to learn and experience what it is like to be unconditionally loved for the first time. I did this without needing to run away from them.

Having experienced my heart opening up in the workshop in Bali, and with the ensuing relationships, I was learning what LOVE is and how it relates to me. This learning process continues to unfold. I had never felt any sort of, what I now believe to be, unconditional Love from anyone in my life. I have no memory of my mother ever holding me or telling me that she loved me or ever showing me any form of love what so ever.

I know that my mother was full of fear and cancer of the womb and internal haemorrhaging from the beatings from my father, so that is the only experience I had of her for the first three years of my life, while she was alive. For me **MUM equalled FEAR and ANXIETY**. So I have grown up attracting people into my life that re-enforced my belief that **LOVE is FEAR and ANXIETY**. It has been one horrendous struggle to find and to experience unconditional Love of any form. Then to have been sexually abused by a man, a male father figure in the orphanage reinforced my other belief that LOVE is always conditional.

This has been a very painful, confusing and stressful journey to uncover my deep-seated beliefs. To discover the shameful and painful feelings buried with the beliefs, and to then grieve the losses associated with them, all so that I could let them go.

I felt such deep grief and sadness around my never knowing what LOVE really was. To have had to learn it at the age of forty-five seemed so hard. I felt that it was UNFAIR that I had never felt unconditional love in my life. There have been times where I have had to hold onto my close friends and God to get me through some days.

I went through four major beliefs about Love:
1) "I am unworthy of unconditional Love"
2) "I am afraid of LOVE"
3) "I am not valued as a human being"
4) "I am worthless"

These all went back to several different events in my life and they all had so much shame and grief attached to them. I have also had the belief come up that "**I don't know how to handle being unconditionally LOVED,**" and this belief has brought up a lot of hurt and pain also.

I am so grateful to the creators of the Process I have been living since 1997. I use this process to help me unhook from these shameful and distressing events and beliefs from my past. I have experienced acknowledgement of my pain and feelings; throughout my healing journey. And on each occasion I wasn't able to feel any sort of response. I just felt numb and even when I tried to let it sink into my being; there was still this nothingness. Whenever I said I loved someone, it felt like I was being a phony and that I was not real. I worked through this belief of **"I am not being real"** and took a new action.

I then travelled to the Gold Coast to work with a Sex Therapist for several days to try and unlock my passion and joy of sex within myself. I also felt that it would help me be able to feel compliments when I got them.

All went well the first two days, but on the third day, when I was feeling most vulnerable, I ended up feeling abused and traumatised by the therapist. She wasn't able to help me when I began to relive my sexual abuse in the physical, emotional and psychological sense. I was re-traumatised and left high and dry, and stuck in the trauma of my childhood.

I had to stop going to her, as I had lost all respect and trust for her and with her. I did feel that the first two days of therapy was helping and gave me hope, but the third day was the opposite. I feel now that she was not skilled nor experienced enough to have been able to help me like she said she could.

She constantly left the room while we were working on crucial moments made me feel abused. She also kept trying to make me responsible for all that she wasn't doing to keep me safe during the sessions with her. Plus the way that she spoke to me was very abusive as well. The tone of her voice was not very respectful and loving.

I left her and went to the beach to recover from my ordeal with her. I processed several beliefs about myself after this experience with the sex therapist and now feel grateful that she did help me unlock the blocks in me. Now I could be free to experience a more fulfilling sexual relationship with a lady in the future.

I have felt *in love* several times in my life, and it has always ended up in a mess, both for me and the other person. The journey for a lasting loving relationship continues with a willingness to be open to LOVE and, more importantly, to being open to the love that is within me and is a part of me.

Reaching out again for support

A new spiritual guide came into my life during my sexual healing stage and has been a great source of friendship and guidance in all areas of my sexual healing and emotional and spiritual growth. He travels the world helping people with severe sexual and spiritual problems. He has been a great role model for me on how to own and nurture my God given sexual energy. I did several workshops on sexual healing with him and I have been to many of his personal lectures on living the spiritual life and how to apply spiritual principles to my own life. While I have felt that he has helped me greatly, he has always said that he has never seen me as a client, but more as a fellow spiritual guide. We supported each other. He guided me to do some work with another American therapist who is now living in Australia.

Releasing my guilt and shame

Several months passed and I enrolled in a workshop with this other therapist now living in Australia. I turned up for the three-day workshop at the Tweed Heads Community Centre. It was a Friday night at about 5 p.m. and there were about fifty people there with a mix of older and younger people; male, and females from all walks of life.

The workshop was to be on releasing emotional energies and learning some grounding exercises for emotional healing. I had been in severe guilt for over two weeks and was in contact with my therapist in the USA. He had suggested that I get in touch with the former American therapist he had previously recommended to me. The workshop focused on healing the guilt. I was carrying a lot of guilt at this time, not knowing where it had come from or how to release it from my body.

I had never felt guilty to this extent before in my life. I felt like ripping my skin off my bones and cutting it off myself. I felt like I was going to die most of those weeks leading up to the workshop. An older lady in the workshop told me, on the last day, that when she saw me on the first night of the workshop she was so scared of me, because of the way I looked to her. She said that I looked really spooky.

I know I was not in a very good space, as I was working through my guilt and I wasn't going to numb these feelings. I felt really proud of myself for staying in an **authentic** space with my feelings of guilt, as I was able to work through them in the workshop.

We shared lots of fears and shame at the start, after we had done some grounding exercises.

We went through lots of grounding exercises throughout the weekend and learned how to access our rage and anger on physical levels, as well as emotionally. Yelling with the men one by one and at the women all grouped together, then having the women do the same back to us men, was so powerful that I ended up not being able to talk. I coughed up blood at the end of that session.

We also learned the pressure points in the jaw, the thighs and knees where we store anger, and then how to release that anger from our bodies. We also used a chair-kicking technique and smashed a big foam ball as ways of getting the anger out. We did some inner-child work with a partner, which was very powerful. To be held by a beautiful young lady while I was sobbing with my inner-child was so empowering for me.

We also did some drama role-plays in small groups, which were really good to feel what it would feel like to be in our other personalities. We learned how to massage and energise other people using our energies.

We all stayed together at the homes of those who were training in the work, with the facilitator, and went through some really shameful stuff—which united us in a very special way. To hear young teenage girls and ladies sharing about their sexual abuse and contracting STD's from the experience, was so inspiring to me. They were all very courageous people.

I had to get the facilitator to work on my jaws doing some pressure point release work on me. He was a giant of a man who was able to help me access and express all the anger and shame and guilt that I could at the time.

We would end the days with prayer and meditations, and start the days with grounding exercises. We would do grounding exercises at each break throughout the day. The days would go from 7a.m til 10 p.m.; they were very full on and intensive. I felt drained by the end of the weekend workshop and was unable to talk much for over two weeks; afterwards, I slowly nurtured myself back into health.

I continued to go to their support group after the workshop to debrief and come down. It helped me with my understanding of what I had gone through and expressed during the three days of workshops.

I then left that circle of people, as I had done what I needed to do with their support. I am so grateful to the facilitator and all the people who were in the workshop for their help and support on this part of my healing journey.

It took me a few weeks of taking things easy after the workshop to recover fully from the emotional releasing I had done during the workshop.

Meeting with and finding Peace with the Church.

During my time recovering from the recent workshop I was contacted by the church.

I had waited for thirteen years for the opportunity to reconcile my resentment with the institution of the Church and all organised religions.

I had two very close friends accompany me to the meeting for some support. I felt that the church was going to have three representatives at the meeting and I it would have been unequal if I had turned up there by myself.

In the meeting, the head of the church was to give me a formal apology for the abuses I had experienced while I was in the care of the church at the boys home. I asked that I speak first so that the all of the church representatives would know the reasons why he was formally apologising to me.

I also wanted to make my amends to the church for holding onto the resentment I had towards them for allowing all the abuse to happen to me.

I started with my apology first.

I apologised to the church for holding onto my resentment for what had happened to me. The church had no idea about what was happening to me while I was in their care. This really took the head of the church by surprise as he was expecting me to be very angry and hostile about what had happened to me, given the circumstances.

Thankfully I had been healed of my past anger. I had done a lot of healing around my experiences in my childhood, so much so that I was able to be peaceful and calm, and balanced while delivering my talk. I knew that it was part of my making peace with the church; I knew I needed to do it so that I would be free of my resentment with the church once and for all.

I felt freed from the resentment from that very moment—and it has stayed that way ever since. I am so grateful for the self help programs, and the process's I had learned to use for myself and all the friends and mentors who have guided and support me in my natural healing journey.

Then I went into sharing my experiences while in the orphanage. I started by speaking about the constant fear I lived with, during the rule of the House parents at the boys home. The whippings with a leather belt, being yelled out to get up in the mornings and then being herded down stairs like animals being whipped with the belt as we went; being rushed to wash our faces and brush our teeth with salt (and not toothpaste), and for being made to fight my mate till he couldn't stand on his feet.

I told them about being made to sit in the middle of the hot summer day in the bitumen tennis court with my wet bed sheets and not move one bit—for what they thought was wetting the bed, but was actually from my sexual abuser. Then I told them about having all the eighty boys marched past me being told that I was a dirty animal and that I was filthy and unclean. I was living on the edge and frightened 24/7 awake or asleep it didn't matter.

Then I talked about the sexual abuse that I tried to tell the House parents about, but was too frightened to do anything, especially after hearing my friend being beating and belted for telling on our abuser.

The shame that we felt at school, where we were considered bad and untrustworthy because we came from the orphanage was hard to accept. Being forced apart from my older brothers when we arrived at the Orphanage, then being told that my brothers were not my brothers anymore, and that I was put with a group of other boys and told that they were going to be my new family, were all the things I told them.

This all seemed to have a very strong impact on the head of the church and the clergy members. I then went on, telling them of the emotional healing I had undertaken for fourteen years; the effects and scars that I had to live with from those experiences—the loss of relationships, the loss of family, the loss of work and educational opportunities, the loss of connection with God, the loss of connection with my own self, the loss of hope and joy in living and many other losses.

They got the full picture of what it was like for me and what I had to do to start healing and have a better life with all my scars of the past.

This then allowed me to feel good about receiving the formal apology from the church. I felt like they understood and knew what they were apologising for. This made me feel good inside.

My friends told me following the meeting that what I said had really affected the head of the church and the other clergy very strongly, and that I had spoken so well.

When the meeting was over I felt drained but somehow felt I had finally completed this issue with the church that I had set out to do. This took place on June 3, 2005.

The negative feelings left me for good and seemed to have a very positive effect on my whole being.

My decision to find natural ways to heal myself from Depression, addictions, co-dependency has lead me to finding a spiritual way of living that continues to grow with each passing day.

I start each day with prayer and meditation and I finish my day with reflection of my day's experiences and a few words of thanks.

I appreciate simple things in life that I once never noticed or acknowledged.

Things like having a nice comfortable bed to sleep in; to not have any nightmares when I do sleep; to have a quality of eight hour sleep every night; to have a peaceful mind; to be able to actually hear what people are saying when I am listening to them speak; to enjoy my food; to have to ability to make decisions; to be free to be able to express how I feel; to have a special partner to share my life with. I could go on for hours about all the positive things that I am grateful for in my life but I will leave it at that for now.

I wish you well in your search for healing and for the most Positive Human Expression you can achieve in this life.

Chapter 10

MY OVERVIEW ON HOW I HEALED MYSELF NATURALLY FROM DEPRESSION AND ADDICTIONS

I would like to say that each of us will take our own paths toward healing. This is mine and I hope that you are helped by my experiences. I went to several Psychiatrists and one said that he couldn't help me, other than that I should go to a self help program to deal with my primary addictions of Alcohol, Work, Love, Sex, Gambling, Prescribed drugs, and People.

I went to go to a Family of Origin Counsellor to do some group-work. She then guided me to a self help program for my Alcohol problem. I also went to a Counsellor to deal with my co-dependency problem; I went to various other self help programs to deal with my care-taking problems, and to deal with my having been sexually abused and raised in neglect and poverty.

I decided to stop gambling, drinking, working and using prescribed drugs all at once. This sent me into a state of paranoia and fear like never before. I felt like I was losing my mind and going insane. I remember blacking out sober while driving my car and nearly ended up crashing into Toowong shopping centre one Thursday night. I began going to up to three self help meetings per day for the first three years before cutting back the meetings to about two to five per week and I continue to do so today.

I focused on making peace with my past and the people in it and to also make peace with myself and God in the process. About three years into my healing journey I started to experience a deep dark depression and chronic fatigue was setting in. My anxiety and anger was coming back and the tools I had at the time were not working for these feelings. I changed mentors and did some more work on myself, but this only gave me temporary relief from my unresolved and painful past. By my fifth Year of healing I was beginning to have suicidal thoughts.

I am so grateful to my close friends; they helped me to move into dealing with my co-dependency and sexual abuse—what I believe to be emotional healing.

I let go of smoking and caffeine after three years of recovery and this brought up painful feelings that I thought

I had dealt with in my steps. But I know now that smoking and caffeine were just coping mechanisms that kept me from facing my inner pains and feelings. They also added to my depression.

I did my inner-child work initially with one therapist and to some degree with others as the need arose. I also went and debriefed my sexual abuse issues within a Safe Men's Group for one year under the guidance of a doctor. I quit working for about eighteen months and in this time I worked on my past emotional issues and myself.

I also went to learn how to play at the relaxation centre. After a year there I started to run my own games nights for adults. During this time I decided to change my career and start my education in the field of Counselling and Communication.

After six years of healing I was asked by a government department to help out with a case against the perpetrator of my sexual abuse, I agreed.

I continued to do workshops on my healing from the sexual abuse and my time in the orphanages. I have tried to create some sort of healthier man for myself. This would give my daughter a better chance in life.

My daughter and I have had a very close but estranged relationship over the past twenty years of her life. I have been a weekend dad for most of her life and this hasn't helped her much throughout her young life. She now has her own troubles and difficulties to have to heal and deal with. I am responsible for my part in her life not being as healthy as I could be, and she is now responsible for what she does about it.

I have used body-workers and massage therapists throughout my healing journey. I've also changed what I eat and drink. I am still working on the sugar and sweets.

I am now in my twentieth Year of healing and I still work at changing my negative beliefs as they come up, and living my spiritual practise daily. Some days I feel the effects of my alcoholism, and when that happens I don't do much and wait till it passes. I really have had to learn how to nurture myself slowly and gently. I also have had to learn how to re-parent myself.

I have used swimming and walking to help along the way, as well as reading, listening to music and going dancing to try and have a little fun along the way. This has all helped to some degree or another.

I go to a few of self-help meetings weekly and love to pass on to others what has been given to me. I have read lots of books and listened to lots of other peoples' stories and experiences; all of which has helped me immensely over the years. I started a private mobile counselling practise back in 1999, which I use to pass on the Emotional Healing Process's and other life skills that I have and currently still use.

I realise now that while most people strive for material and financial success and status in life, I and many other millions like me, struggle and strive daily to live and love. Also, I realise we can live through one more day at peace with ourselves and with the world we live in.

What to do from here.

My hope is that you have gained some hope by reading my life experiences and knowing that you are not alone. No matter how hard life is no matter what background you have come from, there is always hope for a better life. You do not have to struggle alone.

VERY IMPORTANT.

Here is some Information you may want to ask the person you are planning to enlist before enlisting his or her services to heal.

1) How long have they been doing their specific work?
2) What are their Life experiences? Are they like your own?
3) Have they been through what you are going through, or what you are dealing with?
4) How long has it been since they did their own healing?
5) Does the counsellor live the processes and skills in their own life that they want to teach you?
6) What are their educational qualifications?
7) How long will you have to keep coming back till you learn what you need to learn?
8) What will it cost?
9) Are there any natural aides that will be compatible with what you are being taught?

I found this information to be very helpful in my own healing journey when looking for help.

I also believe it is better to get help from someone who has been through what you are going through, and who also has the qualifications and experience to back it up.

Example:
If you want to heal from addictions naturally, seek an addictions expert with the life experience and educational qualifications in your specific addiction. They will teach you the processes and skills you need to heal yourself naturally.

Remember YOU are responsible for your own healing now that you're an adult. Don't **trust blindly** everyone in the helping profession. I have found that asking the questions above is very important if you want to heal and heal permanently. You must get the information to make a safe and informed decision about your own healing.

Here is one of my favourite sayings.

What the *Soul* is after is the highest feeling of *Love* you can imagine. This is the soul's *DESIRE*. This is its *PURPOSE*. The soul is after the *FEELING*. Not the *KNOWLEDGE*, but the *FEELING*. It already has the *KNOWLEDGE*, but knowledge is conceptual. *FEELING* is *EXPERIENTIAL*. The *SOUL* wants to *FEEL* itself and thus know itself in its own experience.

The highest feeling is the experience of *UNITY* with all that is. This is the *GREAT TRUTH* for which the *SOUL* yearns. This is the *FEELING* of *PERFECT LOVE*. Thus for the *SOUL* to experience *PERFECT LOVE* it must experience every *HUMAN FEELING*.

CONCIEVE, CREATE, EXPERIENCE.

(Unknown)

If you have found some identification with what you have just read, and have formed a connection with my experience and want to find out more about what you can do from here, I have a website where you can contact me **www. coreemotionalhealing.com**